Tough Tractors

Blaine Wiseman

WEIGL PUBLISHERS INC.

"Creating Inspired Learning"

www.weigl.com

Published by Weigl Publishers Inc.
350 5th Avenue, 59th Floor
New York, NY 10118
Website: www.weigl.com

Library of Congress Cataloging-in-Publication Data available upon request.
Fax 1-866-44-WEIGL for the attention of the Publishing Records department.

ISBN 978-1-61690-148-6 (hard cover)
ISBN 978-1-61690-149-3 (soft cover)

Printed in the United States of America in North Mankato, Minnesota
1 2 3 4 5 6 7 8 9 0 14 13 12 11 10

052010
WEP264000

Editor: Heather C. Hudak
Design: Terry Paulhus

All of the Internet URLs given in the book were valid at the time of publication. However, due to the dynamic nature of the Internet, some addresses may have changed, or sites may have ceased to exist since publication. While the author and publisher regret any inconvenience this may cause readers, no responsibility for any such changes can be accepted by either the author or the publisher.

Every reasonable effort has been made to trace ownership and to obtain permission to reprint copyright material. The publishers would be pleased to have any errors or omissions brought to their attention so that they may be corrected in subsequent printings.

Weigl acknowledges Getty Images as its primary image supplier for this title.

CONTENTS

What are Tractors?

Have you ever been to a farm and seen a big machine? This may have been a tractor. Tractors are heavy, powerful machines. They help to make work faster and easier. Most tractor work is done **off-road**. Tractors have been used for more than 100 years.

The word "tractor" comes from a **Latin** word that means "to pull."

All Kinds of Tractors

Did you know that there are many types of tractors? Some do farm work. Others are used by people to construct buildings and roads. Soldiers use **armored** tractors to build camps and barriers. Tractors even do work at airports. They pull carts of luggage to airplanes.

Massive Machine

What does a farm tractor look like? Most farm tractors have a large engine at the front of the machine. The driver sits in a **cab** behind the engine. The driver's seat is near the back of the tractor.

The biggest farm tractor in the world is the Big Bud 747. It is 21 feet (6.4 meters) high and weighs 45 tons (40,823 kilograms) when its fuel tanks are full. The Big Bud was built to plow cotton fields in California.

On the Farm

How do tractors help farmers do more work in less time? Farmers use tractors to help plant and harvest their crops. It would take much longer to plant and harvest crops by hand.

Tillers, harrows, and hay balers are a few of the machines a tractor can pull. Tillers tear up soil. Harrows make the ground smooth. Hay balers chop and bundle hay for horses and other animals to eat.

Before tractors, people used animals, such as horses, to pull farm equipment.

On the Job

How can tractors help with construction work? Roadwork crews use tractors to pull heavy **paving** equipment. Roads can be paved faster with a tractor than by hand. They can build more road in less time.

Skid-steer loaders are a kind of construction tractor. They are slightly larger than a car and can lift heavy loads. Some skid-steer loaders have a bucket on the front. The bucket can lift up to 4,000 pounds (1,814 kg).

Tractor Attachments

How do tractors do different jobs? Special parts can be attached to tractors to help them do different kinds of work.

The backhoe loader is a kind of tractor that has attachments. This tractor has a huge shovel on the front of the machine. The shovel is used to pick up large objects. There is a bucket on the back of the tractor. The bucket is used to dig **trenches** and holes.

Fuel It Up

What kind of fuel do tractors use? Most tractors use diesel. Diesel is a thick, oily fuel.

The first tractor engines were built in the 1800s. They were powered by the same type of steam that rises from a boiling kettle.

Make It Work

What makes a tractor move? A tractor has a big, powerful engine. The engine is strong, so the tractor can carry heavy loads.

Engine power is measured in **horsepower**. The biggest John Deere farm tractor has a 530 horsepower engine. It would take 530 horses to do the same amount of work as the engine for this tractor.

The fastest sports cars in the world have about the same amount of horsepower as the biggest John Deere tractor.

Tractor Safety

Did you know that tractors can be dangerous machines? They can have sharp blades, spinning pieces, and hot engines. Tractors have special features to help keep the driver safe.

Tractor drivers sit inside the cab. The cab protects the driver from dust and noise. Cabs have a sturdy frame. The frame keeps the cab from folding in on the driver if the tractor rolls over.

Some tractors do not have a driver. A person enters data into a **GPS** computer. The GPS uses **satellites** to move the machine.

Make Your Own Tractor

Colored pencils
or crayons

Paper

1. If you could design a tractor, what would it look like? Look at the pictures in this book and online to help you decide.

2. Use the colored pencils or crayons to draw the tractor's design.

3. Be sure to include a special attachment for your tractor.

4. Share your big machine with your classmates, friends, or family. Tell them what type of job your tractor is meant to perform.

Find Out More

To learn more about tractors, visit these websites.

Yesterday's Tractors
www.ytmag.com/colorbook/colorbook.htm

PBS Kids
http://pbskids.org/buster/
videos/in_knox_vid.html

John Deere
www.deere.com/en_US/
compinfo/kidscorner/johnny.html

Glossary

armored: covered to protect against weapons and attacks

cab: the enclosed part of a machine in which the driver sits

GPS: Global Positioning System; a system that uses satellites and a receiver to identify an exact location

horsepower: the number of horses it would take to create the same amount of power

Latin: an ancient language used to form many words in English

off-road: to drive off regular paths, streets, or highways on mud, dirt, gravel, or other surfaces

paving: covering the ground with concrete

satellites: devices that provide information from space

trenches: long, narrow ditches

Index